Ethics for Marriage, Family, and Child Counselors

A Commentary on the California Association of Marriage and Family Therapists Ethical Standards

Federico C. Grosso, D.D.S, Ph.D., M.F.C.C.

Federico C. Grosso, DDS, PhD, MFCC
2020 Alameda Padre Serra • Suite 217
Santa Barbara, CA 93103-1756
Tel 805-962-3628
Fax 805-966-2132

First Printing October 1996

Published by
Federico C. Grosso, D.D.S., Ph.D., M.F.C.C.
2020 Alameda Padre Serra, Suite 217
Santa Barbara, CA 93103-1756

Copies may be ordered from
Meredith Boyd
163 Ramona Dr.
San Luis Obispo, CA 93405
Tel 805-543-2704
Fax 805-543-5160

Library of Congress Catalog Card Number: 96-94889
Ethics for California Marriage and Family Therapists: A Commentary on the CAMFT's Ethical Standards
Federico C. Grosso

Includes bibliographical references and index
ISBN 0-9654534-0-5
1. Marriage and family therapists—Professional ethics.
I. Grosso, Federico C.

This book does not represent the views of CAMFT, CAMFT Ethics Committee, or any of its representatives, nor does it represent an official or unofficial statement by CAMFT or any other CAMFT committee or staff. Statements made in this book are the sole responsibility of the author. These statements cannot be definitively relied upon as interpretations of the meaning of the Ethical Code standards or their application to particular situations. The author recommends to the reader that individual consultation with an attorney be made prior to making ethical decisions affecting her or his practice.

Contents

CAMFT Ethical Standards

To all my friends

who made this book happen

Acknowledgement

I would like to acknowledge the contribution of Herb Gravitz, Ph.D. for introducing me to the concept of law and ethics as a viable part of my practice. Ellen Harper, D.D.S., M.A., has given me continuous objectivity when I have needed it. Richard Leslie, J.D., taught me the nuances and subtleties of law and ethics. Jan Rudestam, Ph.D., gave me the opportunity to enjoy teaching law and ethics from a perspective of safety, rather than fear, and Melvin Gravitz, Ph.D., who helped me create a clinical forensic perspective. Drs. Canter, Bennett, Jones, and Nagy's book "Ethics for Psychologists," gave me the idea to create this book for MFCCs. My students at Antioch University in Santa Barbara who supported my concept of "creating therapeutic safety legally and ethically" and served as an effective teaching foundation for this subject. I also wish to thank Meredith Boyd for her editing and technical management of the publication of this book. Thank you all!

Chapter 1

Creating Therapeutic Safety

When I began teaching Professional Ethics and the Law at Antioch University in Santa Barbara, I became aware of a pervasive attitude among students and faculty regarding MFCC ethics and the law. As I explored this further in the professional community, I realized that it was fear about professional malpractice, the CAMFT Code of Ethics, the Board of Behavioral Science Examiners, and applicable California Law that dominated many MFCCs. As I tried to understand this prevailing fear, I became aware that it was related to pre-Tarasoff versus post-Tarasoff dynamics. The Tarasoff ruling by the California Supreme Court in 1976 created a duty for psychotherapists to break confidentiality to protect potential victims from dangerous patients. Many therapists trained pre-Tarasoff were taught that confidentiality between client and therapist was inviolate. During that time, there were few regulations that needed to be followed by therapists. At that point, even having sexual relations with a client had not yet been criminalized. This period exemplified the humanistic approach to therapy where a loving, caring, and sensitive therapist became the role model of creating an effective client-therapist relationship.

The Tarasoff ruling by the California Supreme Court in 1976 fomented a degree of accountability and responsibility never before experienced by therapists. The nature of the therapeutic relationship changed forever. Tarasoff was the key that opened the door to increasing responsibilities placed upon therapists by society, the courts, legislative bodies, and expert witnesses. From that moment on, being a "good" therapist would not be enough to avoid malpractice: relying on sensitivity, empathy, and understanding would no longer be enough to create and maintain an effective therapeutic container. Professional ethics and the law would begin impacting this container for better and for worse.

Society, California law, case law, and CAMFT's Ethical Standards have begun to place increasing levels of therapeutic responsibility upon therapists. *Professional Competence, Therapeutic Duty, Legal/Ethical Standard of Care, Clinical Standard of Care, Scientific Standard of Care, Informed Consent, Duty to Report, Exemptions to Confidentiality,* and *Legally Prudent Documentation* are all part of the current terminology appearing in the legal and scientific literature. These terms create a greater professional accountability for therapists. Society has demonstrated this accountability through an increasing number of malpractice actions against therapists, licensing board accusations, and disciplinary actions against MFCCs. It is understandable that some therapists react to this climate from fear of legal and administrative actions when facing these increasingly complex professional demands in the legal and ethical arena.

I propose that rather than viewing and experiencing the law and CAMFT Ethical Standards as a threat to MFCC practice, they be experienced as a foundation for creating therapeutic safety. The law and CAMFT's Ethical Standards serve as the boundaries for a "playing field" where the therapist can "play" safely within the established boundaries. Society has recognized and established though the law and ethical standards that "playing" outside of these boundaries can be dangerous and hurtful for clients and therapists alike. Not knowing where these "boundaries" lie, what they mean, and how they are applied can cause therapists to make dangerous and hurtful mistakes in their professional environment.

The CAMFT Ethical Standards were created to define the boundaries of safe and effective psychotherapy. Within these standards a built-in system of safety already exists, that when put in operation, can enhance psychotherapy and can prevent dangerous and hurtful mistakes by therapists. Obtaining and documenting appropriate consultation is an inherent part of this preventive safety system. Failing to consult when necessary, and failing to document a consultation appropriately may cause disruption of the safety system and can be a violation of these ethical standards. Society's demands upon therapists for accountability and therapeutic responsibility appear to be developing beyond being able to utilize appropriate clinical skills and abilities (clinical *Standard of Care*). The current demand includes having an up-to-date scientific knowledge base (scientific *Standard of Care*), understanding and applying sound legal and ethical decisions (legal/ethical *Standard of Care)*, and creating a cohesive container where these three standards of care are integrated appropriately.

My purpose in writing this book is to help MFCCs explore the content, the meaning, and some of the more significant applications of the CAMFT Ethical Standards in order to increase safety and stability in clinical practice. I also hope that this book serves as a foundation for exploration of what constitutes appropriate ethical decisions in MFCC practice. Though broad in scope, it is impossible to discuss every possible application of these standards and every possible scenario that can occur in professional life within the confines of this book. I hope this book serves as a tool for understanding the integration of clinical, scientific, and legal/ethical *Standards of Care* with CAMFT's Ethical Standards. Any therapist practicing outside of these standards, though possibly a "good" therapist, may not meet the challenge of practicing successfully in the 21st Century.

Chapter 2

CAMFT Ethical Standard 1

Responsibility to Patients

In developing ethical standards for MFCCs, the California Association of Marriage and Family Therapists established professional responsibility and created safety for therapists and for clients within the therapeutic process. This responsibility is based on an underlying concept that if growth, change, and/or movement is to take place within the therapeutic environment, safety must exist for the client and for the therapist. Ethics are one part of the structure which creates safety. Other parts of the therapeutic structure or container are defined by clinical, scientific, and legal standards of care. I will begin to address the ethics portion of the structure and its impact on the therapeutic container.

> **1. <u>RESPONSIBILITY TO PATIENTS</u>**
> **Marriage and family therapists advance the welfare of families and individuals, respect**

the rights of those persons seeking their assistance, and make reasonable efforts to ensure that their services are used appropriately.

The first section addresses advancing the welfare of families and individuals. This appears to state that the global goal of therapy or counseling is the improvement of the client's state of being. Doing harm to the client is the opposite state of helping the client improve their well-being. It appears that this standard expects that MFCCs will not harm their clients within the therapeutic container. When working with families, the degree of professional responsibility increases, because the family's well-being must be taken into consideration, in addition to the well-being of individual family members. An example might be when a therapist considers recommending to clients that they must cut themselves off from their families when there is no evidence of eminent danger. The therapist would be advised to consider the impact of this clinical intervention on the whole family and consult with objective peers to determine how this clinical action would be compared to the *Standard of Care,* which is "that care that a prudent and reasonable therapist in the community would provide his or her clients."

Respecting clients' rights takes into consideration civil rights as established by the Constitution of the United States and it may also include additional rights established by case law, such as Tarasoff and others.

Expecting the therapist to make reasonable efforts to ensure that services are used appropriately again incorporates *Standard of Care*. The *Standard of Care* continues to be established by clinical and scientific experts in psychology and by legal/ethical guidelines and case law. In court cases, expert witnesses are brought in to educate the court on what constitutes *Standard of Care*. The expert witness will cite journal articles, books, and research which support the appropriateness of a specific treatment modality. For example, if a therapist who used Eye Movement Desensitization and Reprocessing (EMDR) to treat trauma was being sued for malpractice, Dr. Francine Shapiro, the creator of EMDR, would be asked to testify as an expert witness regarding the validity and reliability of this method for treating emotional trauma.

1.1 Marriage and family therapists do not discriminate against or refuse professional services to anyone on the basis of race, religion, national origin, age, sexual orientation, or disability.

This standard establishes that MFCCs should be aware of their personal biases and must take special measures to prevent these biases from interfering with their clinical work. This standard does not state that MFCCs must provide services to every client who comes to their practice because not all MFCCs have the scope of competence to provide services to every client who seeks help. It is appropriate to refer clients when the MFCC does not meet the scope of competence. For example, if a therapist's services were sought by a bilingual and monocultural Hispanic client, the therapist could not deny treatment based on this client's cultural heritage. However, if the therapist did not have an understanding of Hispanic family dynamics, the therapist would do well to refer the client to another therapist with the appropriate level experience with this culture.

> **1.2 Marriage and family therapists are aware of their influential position with respect to patients, and they avoid exploiting the trust and dependency of such persons. Marriage and family therapists, therefore, avoid dual relationships with patients that are reasonably likely to impair professional**

judgment or lead to exploitation. A dual relationship occurs when a therapist and his/her patient engage in a separate and distinct relationship either simultaneously with the therapeutic relationship, or during a reasonable period of time following the termination of the therapeutic relationship. Not all dual relationships are unethical, and some dual relationships cannot be avoided. When a dual relationship cannot be avoided, therapists take appropriate professional precautions to insure that judgment is not impaired and that no exploitation occurs.

Sexual intercourse, sexual contact or sexual intimacy with a patient, or a patient's spouse or partner, during the therapeutic relationship, or during the two years following the termination of the therapeutic relationship, is unethical.

Other acts which would result in unethical dual relationships include, but are not limited to, borrowing money from a patient, hiring a patient, engaging in a business venture with a patient, or engaging in a close personal relationship with a patient.

This standard acknowledges that in a therapeutic relationship, a power differential exists. Clients usually enter into this relationship seeking help or guidance from the therapist and may be in a vulnerable state. Until clients are able to access their own power and establish appropriate boundaries, the clients rely upon the MFCC to provide guidance in making appropriate decisions. To help clients make such decisions, an ethical MFCC is expected to maintain personal and clinical objectivity and avoid taking advantage of the client's vulnerability. Clinical and personal objectivity is lost when the therapist expands the therapeutic container beyond the clinical role by entering into a second non-clinical and harmful dual relationship (a harmful dual relationship exists when exploitation or loss of objectivity takes place) with the client and the client is expected to maintain a relationship of equality with the therapist. The resulting imbalance between the two distinct and unequal relationships tends to confuse clients and create greater dependency on the therapist. Therapists who do not maintain objectivity and/or exploit their clients are likely to harm the client. For example, a client seeks the services of an MFCC because the spouse has been having an affair and the client is confused and hurt. At that moment, the MFCC holds greater power than the client and if the MFCC takes advantage of the client's confusion regarding the status of the marriage and makes sexual advances to the client, the MFCC has lost clinical objectivity and has begun to exploit the client.

This standard accepts the fact that in some locations or in some circumstances, dual relationships cannot be avoided. In these situations, a therapist may take professional precautions by consulting with experts in the legal/ethical arena and documenting the results of the consultation. Therapists living in a small town or who are members of a close-knit ethnic community will face this challenge. Some of these challenges include, but are not limited to, using the services of a bank where the bank manager is a client, seeking medical services from a physician who is also a client, or obtaining physical therapy from a client. In these circumstances it is impossible to avoid relationships with clients. However, the nature of the relationship must be evaluated and managed safely by the therapist. For services that require a greater depth of relationship, which could result in loss of objectivity or exploitation of the client, evaluating each situation carefully and obtaining consultation may provide the best possible solution. An appropriate consultation is obtained from an objective peer.

This standard clearly states that any sexual contact with a current client, spouse, or partner of a client, is unequivocally unethical behavior. The term sexual intimacy extends the sanction to the spoken word and includes verbal sexual harassment. Of all possible harmful dual relationships, a sexual relationship with a client can be the most confusing and destructive to the client. Any sexual relationship with a client, spouse, or partner of a client within two years after termination is also considered unethical behavior. Additionally, terminating the therapeutic relationship in order to have a sexual relationship with a client is also unethical since this clinical action may not advance the welfare of the client.

This standard provides examples of unethical dual relationships. Other examples include, having meals regularly with clients, caring for a client's house or pets while the client is on vacation, or taking a client home to protect them from a satanic coven. As society continues to evolve and new opportunities for social interaction develop, therapists will continue to be challenged with determining the ethics of dual relationships. Richard Leslie, the legal counsel for CAMFT, applies the following maxim to the questions he receives about dual relationships, "If you have to ask, don't do it!" Though some may experience this approach as severe, it surely is preventive in scope.

1.3 Marriage and family therapists do not use their professional relationships with patients to further their own interests.

This section addresses the inherent power differential found in the therapeutic relationship. Clients usually enter therapy or counseling from a perspective of weakness in relation to the therapist. The client may be relating from a perspective of injury, abuse, violation, poor boundaries, etc. This client perspective can set up the therapist in a role of greater power: power to either build trust or to destroy it. It is up to therapists to be aware of their own issues which may cloud objectivity and of those behaviors that arise from lack of objectivity. An example would be a therapist choosing not to refer a client for additional counseling with another therapist who has greater expertise because referring the client would mean loss of income. Another example would be a therapist continuing to see a client in spite of the client's readiness to terminate in order to maintain the therapist's current level of income.

The power imbalance inherent in therapy can lead to loss of objectivity and unconscious hurtful acts toward a client. "Reasonable and prudent" therapists guard against such loss of objectivity and prevent hurtful behaviors by consulting with objective peers and exploring these issues in their own therapy.

> **1.4 Marriage and family therapists respect the right of patients to make decisions and help them to understand the consequences of these decisions. Marriage and family therapists clearly advise their patients that decisions on the status of relationships are the responsibilities of patients.**

This standard establishes that MFCCs must be aware of the power differential in therapy and that the therapeutic process is based on empowering the client. The process of empowering clients consists of serving as a teacher and an appropriate role model to help clients make their own decisions. Every decision contains both positive and negative aspects. When the therapist presents these possibilities to the client for full and careful exploration, the client can explore the benefits and consequences of each possibility before making a choice.

This process can become integrated into the client's decision-making process. Choices about relationships also have rewards and consequences. Staying in a marriage versus seeking divorce is a prime example of possibilities. Only the client can make that decision. The therapist can help the client explore both rewards and consequences fully before the client makes a decision. This leads to true empowerment of the client. The therapist must abstain from making the decision for the client to prevent the client's unconscious dependence on the therapist.

> **1.5 Marriage and family therapists continue therapeutic relationships only as long as it is reasonably clear that patients are benefiting from the relationship. It is unethical to maintain a professional or therapeutic relationship for the sole purpose of financial remuneration to the therapist.**

This standard states that the therapist must be aware of when the therapeutic relationship must be ended. That condition exists when the client is no longer benefiting from therapy or counseling. The therapist must continue to assess for this possibility. Clinical judgment, appropriate clinical records, treatment planning, and consultation with an objective peer may provide the therapist the necessary tools to make this determination. Additionally, this ethical guideline appears to state that continuing the therapeutic relationship for the financial gain of the therapist most likely will incur harm on the client. For example, a client has been seeing an MFCC for several years. The client has received a small inheritance recently and can pay the MFCC's full fee. The MFCC tells the client that therapy will need to be continued since the client is not ready to terminate. Though the client keeps bringing up the subject of termination, the therapist replies with the same answer: "You are not ready to terminate." If the MFCC is making this clinical decision based on the fear of losing income from this client, then the MFCC is acting unethically. The therapist must maintain clinical and personal objectivity to make healthy decisions regarding the client's termination process.

1.6 Marriage and family therapists assist persons in obtaining other therapeutic services if a therapist is unable or unwilling, for appropriate reasons, to provide professional help.

This standard dictates that the therapists have an ethical responsibility to provide appropriate referrals for a person when the therapist chooses not to or cannot provide the requested service. It is recognized that not all persons who call requesting counseling are appropriate for treatment, due to lack of competence by the therapist or the client cannot meet the criteria set by the therapist. This standard creates a responsibility for the therapist to provide the names of other therapists in the community who can help this client. It would be in the best interest of MFCCs to maintain a standardized referral process should they refuse to treat a particular client. Following a standardized and verifiable approach is particularly important when refusing to treat those clients who may take the refusal personally and pursue legal or administrative action against the therapist. Ultimately, it is the client's responsibility to follow through with the referrals.

> **1.7 Marriage and family therapists do not abandon or neglect patients in treatment. If a therapist is unable, for appropriate reasons, to continue to provide professional help, the therapist will assist the patient in making**

reasonable arrangements for continuation of treatment.

This standard creates a responsibility for the therapist to establish a process that safeguards the client's need to continue receiving professional services should a reasonable factor cause interruption of treatment. Such a factor could be the inability of the client to pay for services, lack of client cooperation with treatment, vacation time taken by the therapist, the geographic relocation of the client, and even the death of the therapist. Therapists would be best served by having a written plan for such contingencies should any arise. Additionally, the decision-making process needs to be documented in the client's progress notes, including names of referrals and the circumstances that dictate the need for such a referral. To prevent the therapist's estate from being sued for abandonment, should the therapist die, I direct the reader to research Richard Leslie's excellent articles on this topic. Mr. Leslie is the legal counsel for CAMFT and his articles appear in *The California Therapist.*

1.8 Marriage and family therapists, when treating a family unit(s), carefully consider the inherent conflict that may arise between

the family unit(s) and the individual, and shall preserve the integrity of each component insofar as clinically feasible.

This standard states that when more than one person is being treated, and when a continuing relationship exists among those being treated, the therapist must take several reasonable steps to insure client understanding. The client(s) must be clear as to who is or are the client(s), to whom the therapist owes a clinical duty, what steps the therapist will take to insure that each person forming part of this relational group is protected throughout the therapeutic process, and how that protection will take place. For example, a couple seeks therapy to determine if they will stay together. Through written informed consent, the therapist can clarify that the couple is the client, and that individual records shall be kept should they decide to separate. The therapist can also clarify that the therapeutic duty is owed to the couple until that time that they should decide to separate. Should they separate, the therapeutic duty reverts to each one of them individually. As part of insuring safety for clients, the therapist could have given informed consent. This consent would have clarified the therapist's role should the therapist be called to testify as a witness in court. The therapist's "Secrets Policy" would also be stated at the beginning of therapy, adding further safety to this complicated situation.

1.9 Marriage and family therapists obtain written informed consent from clients before video taping, audio recording, or permitting third party observation.

Videotaping, audio recording, or third party observation will affect the issue of a client's confidentiality both in the present and in the future. In some situations, it may be impossible to determine how the client may be affected. However, this standard places a duty on therapists to clarify with clients the possibilities of how confidentiality may be affected and to establish that the clients understand the possible impact of giving their authorization. The client would need to be informed as to the purpose and use of the instrument, and what population would have access to it. Additionally, the consent needs to be in writing to provide safety for the client and for the therapist.

In summary, CAMFT Ethical Standard 1 establishes the nature of the therapeutic relationship, how that relationship can be harmed, elements of therapeutic duty, and what steps a therapist can take to protect the rights and welfare of the client(s). This section creates the initial boundaries of safety for the therapeutic relationship. It also clarifies the nature of the power differential in the therapeutic relationship and how that power imbalance can be abused.

Chapter 3

CAMFT Ethical Standard 2

Confidentiality

Therapeutic safety is the foundation of effective psychotherapy and counseling. Confidentiality within the therapeutic relationship respects the client's privacy and permits the safe continuation of the therapeutic process. Enacted state law in the mental health field has created a legal framework which continues to evolve and affect the client's privacy. Additionally, professional ethics also affect a client's privacy and appropriate use of these ethical guidelines by MFCCs extends the foundation of safety for the welfare of their clients and themselves.

2. CONFIDENTIALITY

Marriage and family therapists have unique confidentiality problems because the "patient" in a therapeutic relationship may be more than one person. The overriding principle is that marriage

and family therapists respect the confidences of their patient(s).

This section addresses the unique challenge MFCCs face when treating more than one client within the container of the therapeutic relationship and states that MFCCs respect their client(s)' confidentiality as mandated or permitted by law. The clients can be individual members of a family, a couple, or any other group of people (except for group therapy), who seek an MFCC's help in improving their relationship(s). To create safety for everyone, MFCCs can discuss the inherent confidentiality challenge with all involved clients at the beginning of therapy and inform their clients that the confidentiality of everyone will be respected unless the law mandates or permits a breach of confidentiality. Additionally, the process of sharing or withholding private communications with the therapist among intrafamily or intragroup members, also known as the "secrets policy," must be addressed at the beginning of therapy to create clarity and to prevent confusion, anger, and possible feelings of betrayal in the client(s) should confidentiality be breached. As MFCCs clarify and concretize this confidentiality challenge with their clients, preferably by obtaining written informed consent, therapists create a stronger foundation of safety for all parties involved in the therapeutic process.

> **2.1 Marriage and family therapists do not disclose patient confidences, including the names or identities of their patients, to anyone except a) as mandated by law, b) as permitted by law, c) when the marriage and family therapist is a defendant in a civil, criminal or disciplinary action arising from the therapy (in which case patient confidences may only be disclosed in the course of that action), or d) if there is an authorization previously obtained in writing, and then such information may only be revealed in accordance with the terms of the authorization.**

This standard establishes the importance of maintaining confidential the private communications a client shares with an MFCC. In maintaining this privacy, the MFCCs create a safe therapeutic environment in which the client(s) can explore issues with little or no fear of being hurt by the disclosure. However, in some important situations, the law has established that third party safety supersedes the individual client's interests where confidentiality disclosures are mandated or permitted by law. For MFCCs, mandated situations include child abuse reporting requirements (Penal Code 11166-11174), elder abuse reporting requirements (Welfare and Institutions Code 1561015650), dependent adult abuse reporting requirements (Welfare and Institutions Code 15610-15650), and serious threat to harm (Tarasoff vs. Regents of the University of California and Civil Code 43.92). Permitted disclosures include when there is a serious threat of harm to self or others (Evidence Code 1024), when the therapist is defending himself or herself in a legal action that arises from therapy (Evidence Code 1020), and when a valid written release of information (Civil Code Section 56 through 56.37) has been provided to the therapist. Even though these mandated and permitted disclosures of confidentiality exist, it behooves the therapist to be cautious in breaking confidentiality. It is important to evaluate the situation carefully, seek consultation from an objective and experienced peer, substantiate all clinical decisions, document these decisions, and only release information which is pertinent and necessary to address the issue at hand. Thus, a "reasonable and prudent" therapist creates safety for the client(s) and for the therapist.

2.2 In circumstances where more than one person in a family is receiving therapy or treatment, and when a third party seeks information related to any aspect of such treatment, each family member receiving therapy or treatment who is legally competent to execute an authorization must sign the authorization before a marriage and family therapist will disclose information received from any family member.

This standard states that to release any information to anyone outside of the treatment unit (this unit includes all interconnected persons who are seeking therapy with the same MFCC at the same time) an MFCC creates safety by obtaining the appropriate consent to release such information (Civil Code Sections 56 through 56.37). Also, therapists inform their clients at the onset of therapy that they will obtain their consent to release any requested information. Therapists will further clarify that if any person within the unit refuses to give consent, the therapist will owe a therapeutic duty to this unit to withhold the requested information. For example, a family seeks the services of an MFCC to improve interpersonal relationships. In time, the parents decide to divorce and the father wants to introduce the information discussed in therapy to obtain legal custody of the children. If the mother refuses to provide a written release of information to the therapist, the MFCC must protect the confidentiality of the whole family unless directed by a judge to do otherwise.

This standard is important because it creates the foundation of informed consent– discussing with clients at the first session what they can expect from the therapist. Additionally, the concept of therapeutic duty to the treatment unit is created by this standard. If the informed consent is obtained in writing, a firm therapeutic foundation based on safety can be created for the benefit of the client and the therapist.

2.3 Marriage and family therapists use clinical materials in teaching, writing, and public presentations only if a written authorization has been previously obtained in accordance with 2.1 d, or when appropriate steps have been taken to protect patient identity.

This standard dictates that therapists have an ethical responsibility to protect their clients' confidentiality when clinical material will be used in a public manner such as publications, lectures, or teaching. This standard provides two alternatives for the safe use this clinical material. Either a consent in writing can be obtained from a client, or the identity and other identifiable information can be altered to protect the client's identity. Either approach suffices and maintains safety for the client and the therapist.

2.4 Marriage and family therapists maintain patient treatment records consistent with sound clinical practice. Records are stored or disposed in ways that maintain confidentiality.

This standard creates a responsibility for the therapist to follow established definitions of "sound clinical practice." Richard Leslie has written that section 1795 of the Heath and Safety Code indirectly establishes the content of mental health records. He believes, however, that Health and Safety Code 1795 clearly defines the content of the mental health records that must be provided to a client when the client makes a request in writing for these records. When releasing these records to the client, the MFCC must provide the legislated contents, or when not releasing the records, provide a written explanation as to why the records are being denied. Should the MFCC not provide the legislated contents, then the MFCC may be breaking the law.

When storing mental health records, confidentiality must be paramount. This means that records must be kept locked in a cabinet. Richard Leslie recommends keeping records a minimum of seven years after the therapeutic relationship has ended. For clients under 18 years of age, he recommends keeping the records for one year after the 18th birthday and for no less than seven years. To dispose of mental health records and to protect confidentiality, shredding is recommended. Ultimately, the therapist can create client safety by following these established steps to protect a client's confidentiality. I direct the reader to research Richard Leslie's (legal counsel for CAMFT) excellent articles on this topic, which appear in *The California Therapist.*

In summary, CAMFT Ethical Standard 2 establishes the nature of confidentiality, how confidentiality is the basis of trust within the therapeutic relationship, and what steps a therapist can take to safeguard the privacy of his or her client(s). This section creates the initial boundaries of safety for the therapeutic relationship. It also clarifies the nature of the power differential in the therapeutic relationship and how that power imbalance can be abused by the therapist.

Chapter 4

CAMFT Ethical Standard 3

Professional Competence and Integrity

Professional ethics and the law interplay to create therapeutic safety. It is this safety that provides the container where effective therapy and counseling can take place. A therapist's competence addresses another level of therapeutic safety by establishing that the therapist will be prepared to manage the issues at hand. Professional ethics provide safe alternatives should the therapist not have the required level of therapeutic competence to manage the presented issues. A therapist's honesty, fairness, and respect of self and other will contribute to the creation of the therapeutic container of safety.

3. PROFESSIONAL COMPETENCE AND INTEGRITY

Marriage and family therapists maintain high standards of professional competence and integrity.

This section addresses the level of training, experience, and education required of therapists in the areas of practice, teaching, and research. Prior to engaging in any of these three areas within the profession of marriage, family, and child counseling, MFCCs must have developed appropriate levels of competence. A "high" level of competence is defined by the *Standard of Care,* which is that level of competence that a "prudent and reasonable" therapist in the community will employ in providing care for clients. Additionally, honesty, fairness, and respect of self and others will be expected of therapists as clinical members of this profession. Section 3 recognizes that a therapist without appropriate levels of competence in specific professional arenas, such as treating borderline clients, can harm a client severely if the therapist provides professional services without appropriate safeguards. These safeguards might include seeking clinical consultation, guidance, or education from an experienced peer.

3.1 Marriage and family therapists are in violation of this Code and subject to termination of membership, or other appropriate action, if they: a) are convicted of a crime substantially related to their professional qualifications or functions; b) are expelled from or disciplined by other professional organizations; c) have their licenses or certificates suspended or revoked or are otherwise disciplined by regulatory bodies; d) continue to practice when they are no longer competent to practice because they are impaired due to physical or mental causes or the abuse of alcohol or other substances; or e) fail to cooperate with the Association or the Ethics Committee at any point from the inception of an ethical complaint through the completion of all proceedings regarding that complaint.

This standard establishes the importance of maintaining high levels of integrity in professional practice. Integrity includes honesty, fairness, and respectfulness to self and others. When therapists violate their responsibility of professional integrity, they can be disciplined by the professional organization. Resulting discipline could include termination of membership, which could also have disciplinary ramifications with the Board of Behavioral Science Examiners (BBSE). Being convicted of a crime substantially related to the therapist's professional qualifications is one example of lack of respect of self and possibly of lack of respect of others. Such a crime could be committing insurance fraud, misrepresenting the clinical license, or embezzling funds from a non-profit agency where the therapist is employed. Another example of an integrity violation would be disciplinary actions by the BBSE, American Association of Marriage and Family Therapists, or other professional organization. Additional violations would include practicing under the influence of addictive substances, practicing while mentally or physically disabled, where the safety of clients is being jeopardized, or refusing to cooperate with an investigation by CAMFT's Ethics Committee.

Ethically, this section states that therapists have the responsibility of maintaining appropriate clinical safety by managing their own integrity within the confines of therapeutic practice, research, or teaching.

3.2 Marriage and family therapists seek appropriate professional assistance for their professional problems or conflicts that impair work performance or clinical judgment.

This standard dictates that MFCCs monitor their personal life for signs of problems. These problems can include marital or family discord, employment or financial problems, endogenous or exogenous depression, substance abuse or dependence, sexual addiction, major illnesses, or any other life crisis that interferes with work performance or clinical objectivity. When MFCCs recognize such impairments, they must take appropriate measures to ensure the safety of their clients. Appropriate measures include consultation with objective peers, personal therapy, obtaining assistance for substance-impaired professionals, medical help, and if necessary, a leave of absence. For example, an MFCC practicing with an unmanageable bipolar disorder can cause severe harm to a client, especially if clinical decisions are made from the manic phase of the disorder. Such actions are considered unethical. However, if the MFCC takes appropriate medication and the bipolar disorder is managed, nothing in this ethical standard prevents the MFCC from practicing.

Ultimately, it is each MFCC's professional responsibility to ensure the safety of the client by temporarily or permanently limiting, suspending, or terminating professional activities when there is a personal problem that impacts the ability to practice therapy. Additionally, termination of professional activities would require that the MFCC provide for the continuation of professional services for clients through referrals to other qualified therapists and assuring that clients have begun treatment with the new therapist.

3.3 Marriage and family therapists as teachers, supervisors, and researchers maintain high standards of scholarship and present accurate information.

This standard places a responsibility on MFCCs who teach, supervise, and conduct research to stay current with scientific and professional information as it develops. It is up to each MFCC to be responsible for maintaining a "reasonable and prudent" level of competence in each professional skill area. There are several approaches to maintaining a "high" standard of scholarship in these areas. Some of these approaches include, but are not limited to, the following: seeking peer consultation from more experienced professionals, using peer study groups, attending continuing education courses, reading appropriate materials (including journals and texts,) presenting or attending workshops, and teaching at a recognized university. An MFCC who begins to supervise interns without receiving any education and/or training in supervisorial skills, may be practicing unethically.

Additionally, the information presented in teaching, research, and supervision must be scientifically accurate. It must be based on professionally founded knowledge which may be obtained from accepted research, time-based professional experience, theoretical principles, and information from seminars, texts, and journals which are accepted by the profession.

3.4 Marriage and family therapists remain abreast of developments in their field through educational activities and clinical experiences.

This standard creates a responsibility for MFCCs to follow established methods of keeping abreast of scientific knowledge in the profession. Professional competence is enhanced by attending appropriate workshops and seminars, reading refereed journals, reading appropriate books and material, attending conventions organized by accepted professional organizations, obtaining acceptable supervision and/or consultation, and participating in peer study groups. An MFCC who has not taken any additional training since graduating from the master's program, may be acting unethically in this arena.

> **3.5 Marriage and family therapists do not engage in sexual or other harassment or exploitation of patients, students, interns, trainees, supervisees, employees, or colleagues.**

Ethically, this section addresses the power imbalance which may exist in professional relationships. These include relationships with clients, students, interns, trainees, supervisees, employees, or colleagues. This power imbalance is seriously violated through sexual harassment or other forms of harassment or exploitation. The MFCC's responsibility is to avoid a harmful dual relationship in any of the above-mentioned relationships where loss of objectivity or exploitation may take place.

3.6 Marriage and family therapists do not diagnose, treat, or advise on problems beyond the level of their competence as determined by their education, training, and experience.

Section 3.6 strengthens the responsibility of MFCCs to address their level of competence when diagnosing, treating, or advising clients on specific problems. In psychotherapy's rapidly evolving and challenging arenas, MFCCs are not relieved of the duty to protect their clients from lack of competence when providing professional services. It is each MFCC's duty to establish a standard of competence for the issues and problems treated professionally. When the standard of competence in a specific area is inadequate, each MFCC has the duty to obtain additional education, training and/or experience in that area and to document the newly acquired level of competence. For example, a client seeks the help of an MFCC because of a concern that obsessive compulsive disorder (OCD) is causing great stress in his marriage. The MFCC decides to provide marriage therapy without having any experience or training in the management of anxiety disorders. The MFCC is unable to help the client with the obsessive compulsive disorder and the couple decide to divorce. The husband feels betrayed by and angry toward the MFCC and decides to register an administrative complaint. If the MFCC did not pursue education, training, or consultation for the treatment of the OCD, treatment decisions may be considered unethical.

In today's litigious environment, it is not uncommon for an opposing attorney to discredit the treating MFCCs by attacking their scope of competence and presenting evidence of professional incompetence. It behooves MFCCs to maintain accurate records of courses taken, books read, workshops attended, and documented supervision with objective and more experienced peers.

> **3.7 Marriage and family therapists do not generally provide professional services to a person receiving treatment or therapy from another psychotherapist, except by agreement with such other psychotherapist or after the termination of the patient's relationship with the other psychotherapist.**

This section addresses the need to clarify with clients when they are obtaining services from more than one therapist. The primary therapist owes therapeutic duty to the client and part of that duty is to provide an appropriate therapeutic plan of action for the client. This plan may include appropriate referrals to expand the treatment container and, ultimately, the therapist is responsible for overall management of the client's treatment. If a second therapist becomes involved at the request of the client without the knowledge of the primary therapist, overall treatment may be undermined and therapeutic safety may be jeopardized. This section further creates safety by addressing the possibility that if the client is dissatisfied with the primary therapist, it is the client's responsibility to address that dissatisfaction and resolve the therapeutic relationship. Ultimately, that relationship must be terminated before a second therapist may become the primary treating therapist.

3.8 Marriage and family therapists attempt to prevent the distortion or misuse of their clinical and research findings.

This section directs that MFCCs who publish their clinical and/or research results and find that their results have been misinterpreted or distorted through any public media such as publications, lectures, or workshops must take reasonable steps to correct such errors. For example, an MFCC publishes a book regarding treatment for anxiety disorders in children. A media review is extremely favorable but misquotes the therapist. As a result, the MFCC is overwhelmed with new clients and decides not to correct the misquoting and thereby inhibit the flow of new clients. This action would be considered unethical under this standard.

Though it may be difficult, or even impossible, to address every single error, the MFCC must take reasonable steps to make appropriate corrections. These reasonable steps may include letters, telephone calls, private communications, and, if necessary, legal action.

> **3.9 Marriage and family therapists, because of their ability to influence and alter the lives of others, exercise special care when making public their professional recommendations and opinions through testimony or other public statements.**

This section draws attention to the inherent power differential that exists between MFCCs and the general population. This power differential may be explicit or implicit, and, ultimately, each MFCC has the responsibility to manage this responsibility in a safe manner. Making public statements to support a political, social, religious, or financial organization may have both positive and negative repercussions. Before MFCCs make any public endorsements of or public statements about any organization, it behooves them to obtain consultation with appropriate individuals to consider the possible ramifications of this action. An example of unethical conduct would be an MFCC publicly supporting a political candidate and making a statement such as, "Based on my professional experience as a therapist, I know that this person is an excellent politician and would serve our community with integrity. I recommend your approving vote." Section 3.9 does not, however, prevent an MFCC from making supportive statements. It only addresses the need for caution and consultation to determine if making a statement is appropriate conduct for this therapist.

In summary, professional competence and integrity are two important contributory concepts to the creation of therapeutic safety by MFCCs. MFCC ethical guidelines continue to address this issue. Each MFCC in California has the responsibility of creating and maintaining a safe therapeutic container by understanding and applying these standards as MFCC practice continues to expand into the next century.

Chapter 5

CAMFT Ethical Standard 4

Responsibility to Students and Supervisees

MFCCs as teachers and supervisors play an important role in modeling appropriate behavior to their students/supervisees. It is the responsibility of MFCCs to create safety within the relationships that may develop with students and/or supervisees. This relationship between the teacher or supervisor and student or supervisee serves as the foundation for future therapeutic relationships that students or supervisees will have with their clients. Previous ethical standards have defined inappropriate dual relationships. The relationships between MFCCs and their students and/or supervisees can also become such a relationship. These sections address creating safety within this special relationship.

4. <u>RESPONSIBILITY TO STUDENTS AND SUPERVISORS</u>

Marriage and family therapists do not exploit the trust and dependency of students and supervisees.

This section establishes the special relationship that exists between MFCCs who teach and/or supervise trainees and interns. This relationship is based on a power differential where the teacher or supervisor holds the power. The power differential may be enhanced by gender differences, social status, professional standing, or economic status. This section explicitly places the responsibility of respecting this power differential on the MFCC by noting that the MFCC must recognize and manage healthfully the trust and dependency that may exist between student/supervisee and/or teacher/supervisor. Exploiting this trust and/or dependency is a violation of CAMFT's ethical standards. An example of unethical conduct would be an instructor becoming sexually involved with a student or a supervisor becoming emotionally involved with a supervisee.

4.1 Marriage and family therapists are aware of their influential position with respect to students and supervisees, and they avoid exploiting the trust and dependency of such persons. Marriage and family therapists therefore avoid dual relationships that are reasonably likely to impair professional judgment or lead to exploitation. Provision of therapy to students or supervisees is unethical. Provisions of marriage and family therapy supervision to clients is unethical. Sexual intercourse, sexual contact, or sexual intimacy and/or harassment of any kind with students or supervisees is unethical.

This standard clearly establishes the fact that MFCCs who supervise and/or teach hold greater power than their students and/or supervisees. The source and enhancement of this power differential has already been addressed. The MFCC is expected to understand and respect this power differential. The relationship between student/supervisee and/or teacher/supervisor holds the same potential for abuse as a therapeutic relationship. Additionally, the relationship between student/supervisee and/or teacher/supervisor serves as the foundation for role modeling a therapeutic relationship for MFCCs in training. Violating the trust and dependency of this relationship can cause the same harm as violating the therapist-client relationship due to an inappropriate dual relationship where loss of objectivity or exploitation has taken place.

This section explicitly prohibits the creation of inappropriate dual relationships such as having a sexual relationship, performing therapy with students and/or their families, or harassing students or supervisees in any manner. If teachers/supervisors believe they may be vulnerable to developing such a relationship with their student/supervisee, it would be appropriate to obtain necessary consultation and, if necessary, the therapist's own therapy to prevent an injurious situation from developing.

4.2 Marriage and family therapists do not permit students, employees, or supervisees to perform or to hold themselves out as competent to perform professional services beyond their training, level of experience, and competence.

This standard states that MFCCs have an added responsibility when performing supervision. The first responsibility is to understand the *Scope of Competence* as defined by law and ethics; second, to evaluate their supervisee's level of competence in therapeutic areas they will be addressing as a supervisee; and third, to ensure that the supervisee does not exceed each supervisee's level of competence. *Scope of Competence* is addressed by having the knowledge, experience, and training to manage clinical issues faced in counseling. Reading appropriate literature and research, attending workshops and courses, and obtaining appropriate consultation or guidance from a more experienced peer when treating clients outside of scope of competence are appropriate approaches to establish competence. Evaluating a supervisee's level of competence is a continuous process addressed in supervision and documented by attendance records for courses and workshops and lists of books and journals read. Ensuring that the supervisee/employee does not extend beyond each supervisee's level of competence requires that the supervisor continually evaluate the supervisee's training, experience, and knowledge and match clinical challenges accordingly. If a case provides excessive clinical challenges, ultimately it is the responsibility of the supervisor to manage this issue safely for all involved, especially for the client. The supervisor could accomplish this by asking the supervisee to take additional courses, seek additional supervision, obtain appropriate consultation from a more experienced professional, and, if necessary, refer the client to a more knowledgeable counselor.

> **4.3 Marriage and family therapists who act as supervisors are responsible for maintaining the quality of their supervision skills and obtain consultation or supervision for their work as supervisors whenever appropriate.**

This standard dictates that MFCCs who supervise trainees and interns hold the responsibility of evaluating their level of competence. Though at this time explicit guidelines for minimum standards for supervisorial training do not exist, ethics still demand a level of competency from MFCCs who supervise. Additionally, supervisors are expected to determine for themselves the minimum requirements as established by standard of care: what level of experience, training, and knowledge would a reasonable and prudent supervisor have to provide adequate supervision.

If an MFCC agrees to provide supervision for an intern/trainee using, for example, Eye Movement Desensitization and Reprocessing or hypnosis as part of trauma treatment, and the supervisor does not have appropriate training in using this technique, then the MFCC would be in violation of this ethical standard. This standard places upon supervisors the responsibility of determining when their supervisorial skills provide the supervisees with adequate supervision. If this is not the case, supervisors must seek their own consultation or supervision from objective and more experienced peers.

Ultimately, ethical standards place upon MFCCs the responsibility of creating safety for those supervisees who are dependent on the MFCC for the development of clinical skills. The teacher/supervisor and student/supervisee relationship can serve as a role model for the eventual therapist/client therapeutic relationship. Role-modeling a healthy and safe relationship in the early stages of learning by MFCCs will help create similar relationships between the future therapists and their clients.

Chapter 6

CAMFT Ethical Standard 5

Responsibility to Research Participants

MFCCs as researchers play an important role in creating safety for their research participants. It is the responsibility of the MFCC to create safety within this relationship. This relationship extends into several areas including, but not limited to, the *Scope of Competence* of the researcher, obtaining informed consent, respecting confidentiality, and avoiding harmful dual relationships.

5. PROFESSIONAL COMPETENCE AND INTEGRITY

Investigators respect the dignity and protect the welfare of participants in research and are aware of federal and state laws and regulations and professional standards governing the conduct of research.

Conducting research competently requires that MFCCs respect the dignity and welfare of research participants. This involves, but is not limited to, evaluating the research protocol and assuring that 1) participants can give informed consent,
2) participants are debriefed after completing the project,
3) all appropriate elements of confidentiality are protected,
4) participants are assured that the research is conducted ethically by the researchers and/or the assistants, 5) all psychometric tests are scored properly, 6) all applicable laws are followed, 7) cultural differences of the research participants are respected, 8) institutional approval is granted, 9) participants are not exposed to harm, and 10) appropriate consultation is obtained when required.

5.1 Investigators are responsible for making careful examination of ethical acceptability in planning studies. To the extent that services to research participants may be compromised by participation in research, investigators seek the ethical advice of qualified professionals not directly involved in the investigation and observe safeguards to protect the rights of research participants.

This standard establishes the importance of determining if the research project follows ethical guidelines. However, because the researcher may not have the required objectivity to determine if the research participants may be exposed to harm, the researcher has the responsibility to obtain appropriate consultation from a more experienced researcher who can evaluate the project objectively. Of paramount importance is the researcher's level of competence in conducting specific research. If the researcher does not have the required level of competence for this project and does not obtain that competence through consultation, experience, and training, the MFCC may be in violation of this ethical standard. An example that may apply here is the following: an MFCC creates an effective intervention for couples where a spouse is diagnosed with cancer. In his zeal to pursue an investigation of the validity and reliability of this intervention, the researcher omits taking a thorough medical history of the research participants, and accepts candidates who are inappropriate for this study. If the MFCC continues with the project without obtaining consultation on this issue, he may be in violation of this standard.

5.2 Investigators requesting participants' involvement in research inform them of all aspects of the research that might reasonably be expected to influence willingness to participate. Investigators are especially sensitive to the possibility of diminished consent when participants are also receiving clinical services, have impairments which limit understanding and/or communication, or even when participants are children.

This standard states it is the MFCC's responsibility to obtain appropriate informed consent from the research participant. The disclosure of the research project must: be in language that is easy to understand, address all reasonable uncomfortable possibilities that may be encountered in the project, inform the participants that they have the option to decline to participate or withdraw from the project, inform the participants of the implications on the therapeutic relationship between researcher and participant, determine if a previous therapeutic relationship exists and the participant decides to continue or withdraw from the project, discuss the management of confidentiality, set a protocol for debriefing after completion of the project, and answer all questions, within reason, about the project.

> **5.3 Investigators respect participants' freedom to decline participation in or to withdraw from a research study at any time. This obligation requires special thought and consideration when investigators or other members of the research team are in positions of authority or influence over participants. Marriage and family therapists, therefore, make every effort to avoid dual relationships with research participants that could impair professional judgment or increase the risk of exploitation.**

This standard dictates that MFCCs who conduct research must extend the safety container to research participants when they decline participation in or withdraw from the project at any time. The extended safety would assure these individuals that the researcher and/or research assistants would not abuse an existing inherent power differential. This is particularly important when clients, students, or supervisees are involved as potential candidates for the research project. Extending the container of safety requires the MFCC who conducts research to avoid dual relationships with these individuals where loss of objectivity or exploitation could take place. For example, an MFCC who has established a friendship with current students or supervisees and invites them to participate in her research project may be conducting herself unethically under this standard because she may have created a dual relationship which may create exploitation of the students. These students may feel pressured to participate in the research project because failure to do so could impact their friendship with the researcher and could also impact their grades negatively. This MFCC would best not invite to participate in her study those students whom she has already established a dual relationship.

> **5.4 Information obtained about a research participant during the course of an investigation is confidential unless there is an authorization previously obtained in writing. When the possibility exists that others, including family members, may obtain access to such information, this possibility together with the plan for**

protecting confidentiality, is explained as part of the procedure of informed consent.

This standard creates a responsibility for MFCCs conducting research to follow established definitions of maintaining appropriate confidentiality. This includes releasing information only when an appropriate release of information is provided by the research participant. If it is impossible to maintain confidentiality in certain circumstances, the MFCC must inform potential participants that their confidentiality may not be respected and under what circumstances this could take place. Following these steps, the researcher would be providing appropriate information to the potential participants to give informed consent. An example would be when a research participant's identity could be deduced by family members who know that their daughter was involved in a specific research project because their daughter's emotional descriptive characteristics were provided as part of the discussion of the research participants. Allowing this disclosure to take place without informing the participant of the potential breach of confidentiality would be unethical.

In summary, when conducting research, an MFCC must follow ethical standards as discussed in this chapter.

These steps include obtaining informed consent, addressing *Scope of Competence*, preventing harm or injury of the research participants, creating a process allowing participants to terminate involvement with the project, and providing participants with information and debriefment after completion of the project.

Chapter 7

CAMFT Ethical Standard 6

Responsibility to the Profession

The CAMFT ethical guidelines have created a social responsibility for MFCCs extending into their professional and social communities. MFCCs serve as role models of appropriate behavior in arenas where social or professional interaction takes place. As role models, they have the ethical duty to exemplify healthy and appropriate interpersonal social and professional interactions whenever possible.

> 6. <u>RESPONSIBILITY TO THE PROFESSION</u>
>
> **Marriage and family therapists respect the rights and responsibilities of professional colleagues and participate in activities which advance the goals of the profession.**

This section recognizes the differences among MFCCs which may include, but are not limited to, cultural, political, social, economic, religious, and sexual orientation issues. It establishes that MFCCs will respect other professionals' rights to hold personal values and apply them in a healthy way to their own professions. Additionally, this section recognizes that MFCCs also hold inherent responsibilities to their clients and to the profession, and that they shall be given an opportunity to carry out these responsibilities in an effective and professional manner. For example, an MFCC who chooses to advocate politically for HIV-infected clients shall not be prevented from doing so by colleagues who do not want this type of political activity in their community. However, this section does not say that unacceptable professional behavior, such as practicing under the influence of drugs or alcohol, shall be tolerated by other professionals in the community.

This section supports those activities by MFCCs that expand public awareness regarding the practice of marriage, family, and child counseling. These activities include public speaking, television and radio interviews, education, career fairs, publications, and similar activities which enhance public awareness about the profession.

6.1 Marriage and family therapists remain accountable to the standards of the

profession when acting as members or employees of organizations.

This standard establishes that MFCCs hold a responsibility for professional accountability when representing themselves as a member of an organization such as a service club or school board, or when acting as an employee of an organization such as a local non-profit agency or a for-profit organization. This means that confidentiality of clients and clients' issues are respected, dual relationships are avoided, credentials are not misrepresented, state and federal laws applying to the MFCC practice are adhered to, and all applicable CAMFT Ethical Standards are followed. All members of the profession are held to the same degree of ethical accountability regardless of employment situation. An MFCC who is employed by a local non-profit agency providing mental health services would be acting unethically if the MFCC were to become sexually involved with one of the clients of the agency or encourages clients of the agency to sell products as members of a multi-level marketing program (such as Amway, Herbalife, and others) directed by the MFCC.

6.2 Marriage and family therapists assign publication credit to those who have contributed to a publication in proportion to their contribution and in accordance with customary publication practices.

This standard states that MFCCs who publish their work have a responsibility to recognize all participants of the publication regardless of their relative professional status and degree of contribution. However, this does not mean that all individuals who participated in the development of a publication will be given authorship credit. Rather, these individuals can be acknowledged in the footnotes, introduction section, acknowledgment section, and any other pertinent section of the book. Unethical behavior would be represented by an MFCC who describes himself as an author of a book when in reality it was written in cooperation with others.

6.3 Marriage and family therapists who are authors of books or other materials that are published or distributed appropriately cite persons to whom credit for original ideas are due.

This standard dictates that MFCCs have an ethical responsibility to protect the original ideas of other professionals who have either published or are yet to publish. Ethical MFCCs do not plagiarize another's ideas as their own and give due and appropriate credit to others' work. Credit can be given by quoting the exact material and referring to the page number and citing the publication, or when adapting material created by others into a publication, appropriate recognition for intellectual origin must be given. If a therapist were to glean ideas from another book and publish them as the therapist's own, without giving appropriate recognition, this would be an example of unethical behavior.

> **6.4 Marriage and family therapists who are the authors of books or other materials published or distributed by an organization take reasonable precautions to ensure that the organization promotes and advertises the materials accurately and factually.**

This standard creates a responsibility for the MFCC who publishes to prevent the inaccurate promotion and advertisement of published materials by an overzealous marketing department of the publishing organization.

Taking "reasonable precautions" means that the MFCC has consulted previously with the publisher's department and has taken appropriate steps to clarify the intended marketing message that accurately states the content of the publication. Should an advertisement or promotion be inaccurate, the MFCC has the responsibility of contacting the individual(s) responsible for the inaccuracy and formally requesting a correction of the error.

6.5 Marriage and family therapists recognize a responsibility to participate in activities that contribute to a better community and society, including devoting a portion of their professional activity to services for which there is little or no financial return.

Ethically, MFCCs have a social responsibility to provide some form of professional services to their community as pro bono or for small financial remuneration. The intention here is not to give away services, rather it is intended to provide services to those members of the community who are unable to obtain counseling due to their economic or social position. An MFCC can provide these services in different ways including, but not limited to, having some low fee slots, serving as an officer in the local or state CAMFT organization, volunteering as a therapist to a local non-profit counseling organization, providing consultation at no charge to local counseling agencies that utilize interns or trainees, or serving as a volunteer supervisor or consultant to non-profit counseling agencies.

> **6.6 Marriage and family therapists are concerned with developing laws and regulations pertaining to marriage and family therapy that serve the public interest, and with altering such laws and regulations that are not in the public interest.**

Ethically, MFCCs have an obligation to advocate for legislation which would enhance the advancement of family life and for the advancement of marriage and family therapy as an art, a science, and a mental health profession. Monitoring the legislative process of proponents or detractors of such laws, writing letters to individual legislators, becoming involved at the local chapter level, and voting to support or defeat appropriate legislation, are reasonable steps that an MFCC can follow as a member of the profession.

6.7 Marriage and family therapists cooperate with the Ethics Committee and truthfully represent facts to the Ethics Committee.

This section addresses situations arising from complaints made against MFCCs. Any complaint against a member is investigated by the Ethics Committee. Due process is followed as explained in the Ethical Standards for Marriage and Family Therapists Part II. The Ethics Committee expects each member to cooperate fully with an investigation. To protect all parties involved, confidentiality will be respected and legal releases of information will be obtained. Ethically, it is expected that the participating MFCC will be truthful in representing all facts to the Ethics Committee.

Should the Ethics Committee attempt to settle the dispute or make a formal recommendation to the Board of Directors, a participating member is mandated to cooperate fully. Non-compliance of this ethics section can be seen as a serious violation of the CAMFT Ethics Standards and the committee "may appropriately impose more stringent sanctions upon members previously found to have violated the CAMFT Ethical Standards for Marriage and Family Therapists."

Chapter 8

CAMFT Ethical Standard 7

Financial Arrangements

The issue of fees within the therapeutic context can challenge an MFCC's ability to create therapeutic safety. This topic can raise unresolved money issues for both the client and the therapist. Addressing the fee issue immediately and clearly at the onset of therapy helps the MFCC create therapeutic safety. Uncertainty of the future and financial pressures in the mental health field have fomented many dangers which could challenge the therapeutic process. Appropriate use of the ethical guidelines by MFCCs can minimize these dangers and create a foundation of safety for the welfare of their clients and for themselves.

7. <u>FINANCIAL ARRANGEMENTS</u>

Marriage and family therapists make financial arrangements with patients, third

party payors, and supervisees that are understandable and conform to accepted professional practices.

This section addresses the importance of MFCCs managing and clarifying their fee structure with clients. The therapeutic relationship can be experienced as a contractual arrangement which requires that the client must have the competence to give informed consent. It is the responsibility of the MFCC to provide all and *not* withhold any information, which would help the client give informed consent. The exchange of legal tender for services is an acceptable professional practice. MFCCs are free to set their own fees, have sliding fee scales based on financial ability to pay, provide low-fee slots, or even provide free services.

Whatever fees and financial structures MFCCs choose in their practice, they must conform to acceptable professional practices and be structured in form and language that clients can easily understand. Examples of unacceptable professional practices are bartering where exploitation or loss of objectivity may take place, insurance fraud, or allowing clients to accrue large unpaid balances which may create an undue financial burden on the client. Examples of unacceptable professional practices with supervisees are bartering in lieu of providing a salary, charging a fee for providing supervision, or coercing a supervisee to accept an unusually low salary in exchange for having the opportunity to accrue hours toward licensure. Though bartering is not specifically excluded in this section, it can be fraught with danger should loss of objectivity or exploitation take place. An example Richard Leslie gives clarifies the possibility of exploitation. A client gives the therapist a piece of jewelry, though appropriately appraised by a reputable third party, in exchange for services. Should the client feel dissatisfied with the outcome of therapy, the client could accuse the MFCC of taking advantage of his or her emotional vulnerability by taking a "family heirloom".

7.1 Marriage and family therapists do not offer to accept payment for referrals.

This standard identifies the potential abuse of the client's welfare. If an MFCC were to accept or offer a fee for a referral, then the referral would most likely not be made in the best interest of the client. Rather, the MFCC's financial gain would supersede the client's best interest. This standard prevents the possible exploitation of the client and gives MFCCs the responsibility of referring a client to another professional only when the referral would be in the client's best interest. An example of unethical conduct would be MFCCs giving a percentage of their fee to people who refer clients to them.

7.2 Marriage and family therapists will not exploit their patients financially.

This standard attempts to create therapeutic safety by addressing the inherent power differential in the therapeutic relationship, especially when the client may be extremely distraught or may be in an emotionally vulnerable place. MFCCs could exploit clients financially by setting an inflated fee when the clients' emotional or physical state is such that they are unable to competently contract for therapeutic services in their own best interest or when they are emotionally dependent on the therapeutic process for their sense of well-being (such as being depressed or suicidal). Another form of exploitation occurs when MFCCs continue to treat clients for financial reasons without any further benefit to the clients. If an MFCC fails to address termination of therapy when the client is ready, this could be a breach of this ethical standard. Ultimately, this ethical standard expects that the client will be given the opportunity to make a competent decision and give informed consent about the fee being charged.

7.3 Marriage and family therapists disclose their fees at the beginning of services and give reasonable notice of changes in fees.

This standard dictates that therapists have an ethical responsibility to protect their client's ability to give informed consent when contracting for therapeutic services. MFCCs determine their fee structure as long as it is consistent with state law. The MFCC presents the fee to the client, preferably at the first session. There may be reasonable situations where the fee cannot be agreed upon immediately, either because the client is too emotionally distraught to focus on financial matters, or is extremely agitated (when the client faces a crisis issue) to reasonably discuss fees. Clinically, MFCCs would be required to document their judgment and proceed to discuss and come to an agreement regarding the fee with the client as soon as possible.

It is ethically acceptable to increase fees during the course of therapy as long as clients are given a reasonable notice as to when the fee increase will take effect. This expands the need for clients to continue giving informed consent for contractual changes. A "reasonable" length of time is that time that clients would need to determine if they can or cannot pay the new fee. If clients inform the MFCC that they cannot pay the new fee, the MFCC must either continue treatment at the old fee or take reasonable and prudent steps to assure that the client will continue their therapy with another therapist. If an MFCC raises his fees indiscriminately because "the client can afford it," this MFCC would be acting unethically in this arena.

7.4 Marriage and family therapists represent facts truthfully to patients, third party payors, and supervisees regarding services rendered.

This standard creates a responsibility for the MFCC to provide accurate information regarding how fees will apply to therapeutic services. The client must be informed if telephone time will be charged and at what fee, how reports will be charged, and how home visits will be charged. If insurance will be used by the client, the MFCC must be aware of what constitutes insurance fraud. Providing an inappropriate DSM IV code for insurance purposes, double billing the same amount to different insurance companies, billing for missed appointments and identifying these visits as treatment, and billing higher fees to insurance companies are all examples of insurance fraud. I encourage the reader to explore Richard Leslie's excellent articles addressing this subject.

When supervisees are providing clinical care under the supervision of MFCCs, the supervisors have the added responsibility of seeing that the supervisees follow this ethical guideline in the same manner that "reasonable and prudent" MFCCs would follow it. Ultimately, it is the MFCC's responsibility to fully inform her or his clients how services provided will be charged, at what fee, and how to utilize insurance benefits in a manner that is consistent with the law.

Chapter 9

CAMFT Ethical Standard 8

Advertising

Professional advertising within the therapeutic context can challenge an MFCC's ability to create therapeutic safety. When used appropriately, advertising can serve to educate, promote, enhance, and market the MFCC in the community. Conversely, advertising can also be "false, fraudulent, misleading and deceptive" when it is inaccurate, unclear, or a misrepresentation of actual facts. MFCCs continue to strive toward distinctiveness within the profession. When attempting to create such distinction, use of unclear advertising or public statements can create confusion or misunderstanding with potential clients. When the clients make decisions based on false, fraudulent, misleading, or deceptive information, they are not able to provide informed consent to begin the therapeutic process. Appropriate use of the advertising ethical guidelines by an MFCC can provide the basis for clients giving informed consent and create a base of safety within the therapeutic and professional context.

8. ADVERTISING

Marriage and family therapists engage in appropriate informational activities, including those that enable lay persons to choose professional services on an informed basis.

This section addresses the importance of using appropriate vehicles to disseminate information describing the MFCC's professional foundation. These communications may take the form of education, advertising, marketing, promotion, and statements made by others. The MFCC may use business cards, brochures, newspaper, radio and television advertisement, yellow pages, etc., as long as the information contained is accurate, clear, and honest. Inappropriate advertisement activities would involve paying finder's fees to advertisers for each new client obtained as a result of the advertising, or soliciting testimonials from clients to market the therapist. It is the MFCC's responsibility to avoid fraudulent, deceptive, misleading, or false communications which may misinform potential and current clients about the MFCC. It is the MFCC's responsibility to provide clients with clear, accurate, and honest information allowing them to choose professional services from an informed perspective, and thereby, allowing clients to give true informed consent at the beginning of the counseling process.

> **8.1 Marriage and family therapists accurately represent their competence, education, training, and experience relevant to their professional practice.**

This section enhances the importance of providing potential clients and the community at large an accurate presentation of skills, education, training, knowledge, and abilities, otherwise known as professional competence. Clients can choose an appropriate MFCC for services, when they have the ability to make an informed choice. This choice must be based on accurate and sound information. An example of a violation would be MFCCs without degrees in clinical psychology representing themselves as psychologists. Another ethical violation would be MFCCs describing themselves as specialists without the educational and experiential basis to make such a claim. Ethically, MFCCs must provide accurate and sound information about themselves to help clients make informed decisions.

> **8.2 Marriage and family therapists assure that advertisements and publications, whether in directories, announcement cards, newspapers, or on radio or television, are formulated to accurately convey information that is necessary for the public to make an appropriate selection.**

This section addresses the importance of providing true, accurate, and honest communications when using the media to disseminate information describing the MFCC's professional foundation. The MFCC may use business cards, brochures, newspaper ads, publications, radio and television advertisement, yellow pages, etc., as long as the information contained is accurate, clear, and honest. If an advertisement, brochure, radio spot, television ad, or any other form of advertisement is incorrect, it is the responsibility of the MFCC to address and correct the error. If the material has already been printed, it is the responsibility of the MFCC to stop the dissemination of misleading material and to discard it in such manner that prevents its future utilization. It is the MFCC's responsibility to provide honest, clear, and accurate information to clients regarding their qualifications and experience. This action allows clients to choose professional services from an informed stance. If an MFCC allows a successful yet misleading radio commercial to continue without correcting it because it provides a continuous flow of new clients, this would be an example of unethical conduct.

> **8.3 Marriage and family therapists do not use a name which could mislead the public concerning the identity, responsibility, source, and status of those practicing under that name and do not hold themselves out as being partners or associates of a firm if they are not.**

This standard dictates that MFCCs must be clear, honest, and accurate in the representation of the ownership of their practice that provides services to their clients. Clients must have the ability to determine who they are receiving clinical services from and who is responsible for the quality of care provided. Should a question arise regarding the services provided, the client must know how to reach that person to seek redress. If a fictitious name is chosen for the place of business, legally the client must be informed at the onset of therapy who is/are the owner(s) of the registered place of business.

This standard also addresses the need for clarity in describing the affiliations within and ownership of a practice or place of business. It is unethical for MFCCs to describe themselves as partners or associates in a business when in reality they may be employees. An example of a violation of this standard may be when an MFCC states to the client that he or she is a partner of the "Psychological Offices of Dr. Smith," when in reality the therapist is only an employee. Additionally, using the name "psychological offices" may be misleading since it may imply that the place of business is a psychologist's office and the MFCC does not have such a license. Clarity in this issue can prevent misunderstandings and potential problems for the MFCC.

8.4 Marriage and family therapists do not use any professional identification (such as a business card, office sign, letterhead, or telephone or association directory listing) if it includes a statement or claim that is false, fraudulent, misleading, or deceptive. A

statement is false, fraudulent, misleading, or deceptive if it a) contains a material misrepresentation of facts; b) fails to state any material fact necessary to make the statement, in light of all circumstances, not misleading; or c) is intended to or is likely to create an unjustified expectation.

This standard addresses the nature of a false, fraudulent, misleading, or deceptive statement. A statement can be false, fraudulent, misleading, or deceptive by omission and commission. Adding or detracting from a statement can change its inherent message. If a statement modifies the facts enough to make it false, is missing facts which would make the statement true, or creates an expectation in the client which cannot be fulfilled, then the statement can be considered false, misleading, fraudulent, or deceptive. Some examples of unethical behavior are MFCCs listing publications that they did not write (adding their names to commercially available articles and publishing them in newspapers as their own), adding a degree to their name that they do not possess, describing themselves as specialists when they have not indeed had specialized training, using the CAMFT logo on business cards without being members of

CAMFT without written authorization from CAMFT's board of directors. Ultimately, it is the MFCC's responsibility to prevent such errors of omission or commission by scrutinizing all written materials which will be used to disseminate information about the practitioner.

8.5 Marriage and family therapists correct, wherever possible, false, misleading, or inaccurate information and representations made by others concerning the therapist's qualifications, services, or products.

When MFCCs become aware of any incorrect information in written or spoken disseminated information about themselves, they have the ethical responsibility to take reasonable steps to correct the error. Reasonable steps would mean informing those responsible for the omission of the information or inclusion of the erroneous data that the incomplete or incorrect information must be changed. If the material has been printed, the MFCC would take appropriate steps to prevent the dissemination of the erroneous publication. If the material is spoken, a letter to the responsible party indicating the necessary corrections would be appropriate.

It is understood that not all circumstances where errors occur can be changed. However, the MFCC must take reasonable steps to prevent the repetition of false, misleading, or inaccurate information.

8.6 Marriage and family therapists make certain that the qualifications of persons in their employ are represented in a manner that is not false, misleading, or deceptive.

MFCCs employing interns or licensed MFCCs must take the precaution of verifying the licensure or registration status of their employees. Additionally, all written and spoken information indicating the licensure status and competence of their employees must be accurate, honest, and clear. Ethical violations of this section would include introducing a registered intern as a licensed MFCC, stating that the registered intern has the competence and training in working with special situations even though the intern has not had such training or experience, or exaggerating the experience of an employee who is a licensed MFCC to make them "look good" to clients. The employer is ultimately responsible for preventing misleading, false, or deceptive representation of the qualifications and competence of her or his employees.

> **8.7 Marriage and family therapists may represent themselves as specializing within a limited area of marriage and family therapy, but only if they have the education, training, and experience which meet recognized professional standards to practice in that specialty area.**

Ethically, MFCCs who identify themselves as "specialists" must follow guidelines set for specialty status by recognized boards or academies. These organizations require a specific number of years of clinical experience, a literature knowledge base for the specialty area, a set number of hours of continuing education in this arena, and a comprehensive examination before individuals will be certified as specialists. Because MFCCs state that they have specific areas of interest in their practice and treats these areas does not make them "specialists."

There are areas of MFCC practice that do not have recognized specialties. Ethical MFCCs would seek a comparable specialty board in psychology and follow a parallel course of study, training, and experience before calling themselves specialists. It is the responsibility of all MFCCs to have the knowledge base, training, and experience in the treatment issue or area of practice before they can call themselves specialists.

> **8.8 CAMFT clinical, associate and prelicensed members may identify such membership in CAMFT in public information or advertising materials, but they must clearly and accurately represent whether they are clinical, associate, or prelicensed members.**

The California Association of Marriage and Family Therapists allows members to identify themselves as belonging to the professional organization as long as they correctly identify their membership status. Currently, CAMFT recognizes three separate categories: a) clinical members, which includes all members who have been licensed by the Board of Behavioral Science Examiners in California and who are licensed as MFCCs, b) associate members, which includes all individuals who wish to join CAMFT and are not licensed MFCCs or are in the process of obtaining their licensure, and c) prelicensed members, which includes all members who are registered interns or trainees.

8.9 Marriage and family therapists may not use the initials CAMFT following their name in the manner of an academic degree.

It is unethical for members of CAMFT to add the initials "CAMFT" to their name as if they represented an academic degree. Doing so would be misleading since any reasonable person could assume that these initials represented a formal degree.

8.10 Marriage and family therapists may use the CAMFT logo only after receiving permission in writing from the Association. Permission will be granted by the Association to CAMFT members in good standing in accordance with Association policy on use of CAMFT logo. The Association (which is the sole owner of its name, logo, and the abbreviated initials CAMFT) may grant permission to CAMFT committees and chartered chapters in good standing, operating as such, to use the CAMFT logo.

> **Such permission will be granted in accordance with Association policy on use of the CAMFT logo.**

Members of CAMFT who are in good standing may include the CAMFT logo in their professional presentations, which includes business cards, letterhead, advertising or in a directory as long as a) the request is made in writing to the Association, b) a statement is made that the user will include the words "California Association of Marriage and Family Therapists" with the logo including the category of membership, c) the statement describes where the logo will be used (letterhead, advertising, etc.), d) the request is accompanied by a copy or copies of the final product(s), and e) the recipient has obtained written authorization from the Association prior to use of the logo. An MFCC who does not follow the policy on use of the logo as defined by CAMFT is in violation of this ethical standard.

CAMFT chapters may use the logo when they are duly chartered by the Association and when the logo will be used for official chapter business, such as letterhead, advertising, leaflets, and brochures. The chapter officers would follow CAMFT's policy on use of the logo prior to official use. It would be unethical for a chapter to use the

CAMFT's logo in conjunction with any other logo from any other organization. Such use would imply official sanction of CAMFT for the second organization. This action would be a misrepresentation of fact.

8.11 Marriage and family therapists use their membership in CAMFT only in connection with their clinical and professional activities.

It is unethical for any members of CAMFT to utilize their membership in CAMFT in any arena outside of clinical and professional activities. An example of unethical conduct would be MFCCs who are running for office for a local school board state in their ad campaign literature that they are members in good standing of CAMFT. This would imply that CAMFT has given this MFCC official sanction for his or her personal activities. This action would be a misrepresentation of fact.

CAMFT Ethical Standard 8 establishes the nature of clear, honest, correct, and proper advertising and public communications. Any deviation from these can lead to false, fraudulent, misleading, or deceptive professional communications which can adversely affect the therapeutic relationship and process. Additionally, this section creates additional boundaries of safety for the therapeutic container.

Chapter 10

Managing Ethical Challenges Safely

MFCCs are facing a greater number of challenges in the profession. Managed care, increasing number of therapists competing for the same market, repressed memories, greater vigilance and control by the licensing board, increasing malpractice actions, and an increasing number of complaints filed with the BBSE and Ethics Committees all make clinical practice an ongoing challenge. Some therapists have decided to change professions. Others practice from a position of fear, worrying about attorneys and the BBSE. Sadly, these approaches are based on fear of the worst case scenarios and may lead to a lack of enjoyment of clinical practice. The following approaches come from a different perspective:

A. *Transform fear of the ethical issues into a container of safety.* I have proposed a different perspective to clinical practice: one based on creating safety. This approach relates to ethical guidelines and the law as boundaries which create a foundation of safety for clinical practice. State law, case law and CAMFT's ethical guidelines serve as the container of a safe therapeutic practice. As in a game where the ball lands outside the playing boundaries, law and ethics also create similar boundaries. This approach helps the therapist become free of fear-based injunctions and helps open up opportunities to relate differently and freely to ethics and the law. There is greater personal freedom in asking "How can I create safety for my client?" rather than asking "What do I need to do to protect myself?"

B. *Know, explore and discuss ethical standards with knowledgeable peers.* Expanding the safety container means that the "reasonable and prudent" MFCC will also know CAMFT's Ethical Standards and apply them appropriately. Exploring and discussing them with informed peers helps generate familiarity with the ethical standards should a challenging ethical issue arise. "Be prepared!" is the Boy Scout motto and it is also applicable in the practice of marriage and family counseling.

C. *Know all applicable state and federal laws.* Since the Tarasoff case law became effective, there have an increasing number of state and federal regulations impacting the practice of marriage and family counseling. With new clinical challenges come new laws. Sometimes it is difficult to keep track of every new regulation. Richard Leslie's articles in *The California Therapist* are an excellent resource to track new developments in the legislative arena. As of January 1, 1997, MFCCs will be expected to accrue continuing education credits toward licensure. Though legal and ethical coursework has not been required, it behooves reasonable and prudent MFCCs to stay abreast of current and continuing developments in this area of professional practice. In the court of law, ignorance of the law is not an excuse for unprofessional conduct.

D. *Recognize personal countertransference issues which could lead to potential ethical challenges.* Ethically, an MFCC is expected to be aware of personal biases, preconceptions, weaknesses, belief systems, and limitations which could create lack of objectivity of a professional treatment issue or situation. This insight helps create additional safety within the therapeutic container: the more MFCCs know themselves, the greater freedom they have to avoid difficult and challenging ethical situations which could lead to potential unethical conduct. For additional information, I invite the reader to explore my article titled "Avoiding the Transference-Countertransference Confrontation Trap," (see Appendix A).

E. *Create a personal structure to prevent potential ethical conflicts.* Some relevant questions that a "prudent and reasonable "MFCC may ask herself or himself follow: (1) Is this case addressing *interpersonal* relationship issues? (Scope of Practice), (2) Do I have the training, experience, and education to address the treatment issues in this case? (Scope of Competence), (3) Am I maintaining confidentiality except as permitted or mandated by law including addressing my "secrets policy" and using appropriate release(s) of information? (Confidentiality/Privilege), (4) Am I addressing crisis issues as permitted or mandated by law? (Evidence Code 1024, Welfare and Institutions Code 5150, Welfare and Institutions Code 15630 & 9380, Penal Code 11165-11174, Tarasoff case law and Civil Code 43.92, Bellah v. Greenson, etc.), (5) Am I addressing management practice issues appropriately? (fees, insurance, Health Code 1795, termination, referrals, etc.), (6) Am I avoiding and preventing dual relationships where I will lose objectivity or exploit my client(s)? (Business and Professions Code 729).

F. *Practice within the legal/ethical, clinical, and scientific standards of care.* Know the scientific literature to understand the advantages and disadvantages, strengths and weaknesses of applied clinical modalities and interventions, utilized psychotherapeutic theories, information given to clients regarding treatment, and what the experts say about specific clinical treatment approaches.

G. *Consult with peers and experts who know the application of the law and ethical standards.* Richard Leslie is an excellent professional resource for members of CAMFT. For those who are not members of CAMFT, attorneys specializing in this area are available for consultation. Ultimately, it is the responsibility of each MFCC to seek appropriate consultation when faced with an ethical challenge which could cause potential harm to a client.

As a friend of mine has reminded me on several occasions "measure twice, cut once!" Once the decision has been made and action taken, it is very difficult to change the course of events that ensue, especially if the client is harmed as a result of the action taken. If MFCCs do not deliberately create and maintain a container of safety for their clients, ultimately the licensing board will take appropriate and restrictive steps to create safety for the consumers of the state. It is the responsibility of each therapist to create safety in the practice of marriage and family counseling. By diligently creating this container of safety, all MFCCs have the opportunity to enjoy their practice.

Chapter 11

Future Ethical Considerations

The practice of marriage, family, and child counseling is expanding into uncharted territories. Though the Legal Scope of Practice for MFCCs (Business and Professions Code 4980.02) addresses the improvement of relationships, this is not a limitation of practice, rather it serves as a strong foundation to provide therapeutic and counseling services in many arenas. Such arenas including individual, couples, family, and group counseling; divorce counseling; adoption counseling; custody evaluations; divorce mediation; business relationship enhancement; workers' compensation; teaching; conflict mediation; psychotherapeutic testing; consulting; media and telecommunications psychotherapy; and, forensics and expert witnesses. In the near future, MFCCs can anticipate providing services in the state correctional departments; providing services through Medicare; and if psychologists become licensed to prescribe psychotropic medication, MFCCs will be expected to do the same when the nature of the problem is based on a relationship issue.

Some of these arenas have not been addressed in CAMFT's Ethical Standards. Their omission only means that, as of yet, these issues have not reached a critical mass of ethical challenges in the profession as a whole. As increasing numbers of MFCCs become involved in these arenas and ethical issues arise, CAMFT will begin to address some of these ethical challenges.

The management of psychotherapeutic testing is an area that currently challenges MFCCs. In 1984, the Attorney General ruled that MFCCs could utilize psychometric instruments in their practice when the testing was utilized for the enhancement of relationships. However, those MFCCs using these instruments have not had an ethical obligation to maintain test security, especially when the material was subpoenaed in a legal case. At this time, psychologists can refuse to release test materials to anyone other than another professional qualified to review the test results. MFCCs would benefit professionally should an ethical standard clarify test protection.

MFCCs have begun to develop forensic activities as part of their professional activities. These include performing custody evaluations, consultations with attorneys, forensic evaluations, and serving as expert witnesses. Some of the potential ethical conflicts, such as dual relationships and scope of competence, are addressed in CAMFT's Ethical Standards. However, greater clarity could be gleaned in these activities if specific standards were to address forensic activities. These standards might include a definition of forensic activities, making ethical forensic assessments and recommendations, addressing the nature of validity and reliability of work product, clarifying role as fact witness or expert witness and impact on confidentiality, and disclosing possible conflicts of interest. Such clarification might provide a foundation of safety for forensic activities by MFCCs as they increase their activities in this arena.

Another emerging field is the involvement of MFCCs in media and telecommunications, including telephone counseling and use of the Internet. As this technological field continues to evolve, future ethical challenges may need to be addressed through well-defined ethical guidelines. Richard Leslie has written an excellent article on this subject (November/December issue of *The Therapist).* Currently, there is a lack of information available to determine how market forces will direct the evolution of these nascent arenas for MFCCs.

CAMFT and CAMFT's Ethics Committee have shown vision and patience when addressing ethical challenges. Some years ago, the issue of informed consent was being considered for inclusion into the ethical standards. Rather than acting impulsively, CAMFT judiciously sent out a survey to its members to consider input from its membership. The general membership did not feel that it was ready to integrate this concept into the ethical standards at that time, and CAMFT's Board of Directors did not pursue the matter beyond publishing the results of the general members. As society and market forces continue placing greater responsibility on MFCCs, I believe that the Ethics Committee will renew their exploration of this issue in the future as deemed necessary.

Appendix A

References

Appelbaum, P. S., & Gutheil, T. G. (1991). *Clinical Handbook of Psychiatry and the Law.* Baltimore, MD: Williams & Wilkins.

Bersoff, D. N. (1995). *Ethical Conflicts in Psychology.* Washington, DC: American Psychological Association.

California Association of Marriage and Family Therapists. (1992). *Ethical Standards for Marriage and Family Therapist, Part I.* San Diego, CA: Author.

California Association of Marriage and Family Therapists. (1992). *Ethical Standards for Marriage and Family Therapist, Part II.* San Diego, CA: Author.

California Association of Marriage and Family Therapists. (1987). *The Association's Policy on Use of Logo.* San Diego, CA: Author.

Canter, M. C., et al. (1995). *Ethics for Psychologists: A Commentary on the APA Ethics Code.* Washington, DC: American Psychological Association.

Caudill, O. B., & Pope, K. S. (1995). *Law and Mental Health Professionals: California.* Washington, DC: American Psychological Association.

Corey, G., et al. (1993). *Issues and Ethics in the Helping Professions.* Pacific Grove, CA: Brooks/Cole Publishing Company.

Dickson, D. T. (1995). *Law in the Health and Human Services: Guide for Social Workers, Psychologists, Psychiatrists, and Related Professionals.* New York, NY: The Free Press.

Grosso, F. C. (1995, February). *Standard of Care Versus Standard Care.* Newsletter of the Santa Barbara Chapter of the California Association of Marriage and Family Therapists.

Grosso, F. C. (1995, March). *Therapeutic Duty.* Newsletter of the Santa Barbara Chapter of the California Association of Marriage and Family Therapists.

Grosso, F. C. (1995, May). *Informed Consent: What Is It?* L. A. Therapist Update, Newsletter of the Los Angeles Chapter of the California Association of Marriage and Family Therapists.

Grosso, F. C. (1995, May). *Standard of Care Versus Standard Care.* Santa Barbara Chapter of CAMFT Newsletter.

Grosso, F. C. (1995, June). *The Suicidal Patient: Clinical, Legal, and Scientific Standard of Care.* L. A. Therapist Update, Newsletter of the Los Angeles Chapter of the California Association of Marriage and Family Therapists.

Grosso, F. C. (1995, October). *Professional Competence.* L. A. Therapist Update, Newsletter of the Los Angeles Chapter of the California Association of Marriage and Family Therapists.

Grosso, F. C. (1995, August). *Mental Health Records and Notetaking: Creating Safety.* L. A. Therapist Update, Newsletter of the Los Angeles Chapter of the California Association of Marriage and Family Therapists.

Grosso, F. C. (1995, September). *The 21st Century: Being a Good Therapist Won't Be Enough to Avoid Malpractice.* L. A. Therapist Update, Newsletter of the Los Angeles Chapter of the California Association of Marriage and Family Therapists.

Grosso, F. C. (1996, January/February). *Mental Health Records and Notetaking.* L. A. Therapist Update, Newsletter of the Los Angeles Chapter of the California Association of Marriage and Family Therapists.

Grosso, F. C. (1996). Avoiding the "Transference-Countertransference Confrontation Trap." *The California Therapist,* Publication pending.

Haas, L. J., & Malouf, J. L. (1989). *Keeping Up the Good Work: A Practitioner's Guide to Mental Health Ethics.* Sarasota, FL: Professional Resource Exchange, Inc.

Leslie, R. S. (1983, January/February). Nutritional Advice. *The California Therapist.*

Leslie, R. S. (1989, July/August). Confidentiality. *The California Therapist,* pp. 35-36.

Leslie, R. S. (1989, January/February). Authorization to Release Information. *The California Therapist,* pp. 45-46.

Leslie, R. S. (1989, September/October). Dual Relationships: The Legal View. *The California Therapist,* pp. 9-11.

Leslie, R. S. (1989, September/October). Patient Access to Records. *The California Therapist,* pp. 25-26.

Leslie, R. S. (1990, May/June). Advertising: A Legal and Ethical Perspective. *The California Therapist,* pp. 7-16.

Leslie, R. S. (1990, November/December). Recent Court Decisions Establish Immunity: Custody Evaluations, Mediation Affected. *The California Therapist,* pp. 37-39.

Leslie, R. S. (1991). Recent Rulings Shed Light on "Tarasoff Warnings." *The California Therapist,* 13(6), 25-27.

Leslie, R. S. (1992). Information/Disclosure Statements: Informed Consent. *The California Therapist,* pp. 7-8.

Leslie, R. S. (1993). Ethical Standards. *The California Therapist,* 5(13), 24-25.

Leslie, R. S. (1993). The Relationship Sours. *The California Therapist,* 5(4), 29-31.

Leslie, R. S. (1993). Telephone Counseling Services. *The California Therapist,* 5(6), 40-42.

Leslie, R. S. (1994). Retaining Clinical Records: Problems and Considerations. *The California Therapist,* 6(2), 11-15.

Leslie, R. S. (1994). Managed Care: Ethical and Legal Considerations in Appealing Adverse UR Decisions. *The California Therapist,* 6(2), 24-29.

Leslie, R. S. (1994). Child and Sexual Abuse Repressed Memories—Real or Imagined?: Staying Clear of Unethical Behavior. *The California Therapist,* 6(1), 22-25.

Myers, J. E. (1992). *Legal Issues in Child Abuse and Neglect.* Newbury Park, CA: Sage Publications.

Nurcome, B., & Partlett, D. F. (1994). *Child Mental Health and the Law.* New York, NY: The Free Press.

Rave, E. J. & Larsen, C. C. (1995). *Ethical Decision Making in Therapy: Feminist Perspectives.* New York, NY: The Guilford Press.

Riemersma, M. (1989, January/February). Intern/Trainees: Not Independent Contractors. *The California Therapist,* pp. 16-17.

Riemersma, M. (1990, November/December). What is Insurance Fraud?. *The California Therapist,* pp. 21-24.

Riemersma, M. (1992) The Dos and Don'ts of Interviewing Interns and Trainees. *The California Therapist,* 4(3), 13-15.

Woody, R. H. (1988). *Fifty Ways to Avoid Malpractice: A Guidebook for Mental Health Professionals.* Sarasota, FL: Professional Resource Exchange, Inc.

VandeCreek, L., & Knapp, S. (1993)*Tarasoff and Beyond: Legal and Clinical Considerations in the Treatment of Life-Endangering Patients.* Sarasota, FL: Professional Resource Press.

Appendix B

INDEX

Appendix C

About the Author

Federico C. Grosso, D.D.S., Ph.D., M.F.C.C., is a licensed marriage, family, and child counselor in private practice in Santa Barbara, California. He is a board-certified pediatric dentist who retired from Dentistry due to a career-disabling accident. Currently, he is a member of the department of psychiatry and the peer review committee for allied health professionals at Cottage Hospital in Santa Barbara, California. He is an adjunct faculty member of Antioch University in Santa Barbara, California, where he teaches *Professional Ethics and the Law*. He writes the regularly published column *The Legal and Ethical Corner* for the Los Angeles, Ventura, Long Beach, San Luis Obispo, and Santa Barbara Chapters of CAMFT. He has published several articles in professional journals and has lectured on varied legal and ethical issues and practice enhancement.

Dr. Grosso is an expert in the area of legal and ethical guidelines for California marriage, family and child counselors and serves as an expert witness in this field. He is also a forensic evaluator for sexual abuse and sexual harassment. He is a Diplomate of the American Board of Forensic Examiners and of the American Board of Forensic Medicine. He also consults with attorneys and their clients, who have been severely injured in accidents. Dr. Grosso serves as a consultant on business relations enhancement.